swim   into the north's blue eye

Also by Annette Lapointe

Novels
Stolen (Giller Prize Longlist)
Whitetail Shooting Gallery
... And This Is the Cure

Stories
You Are Not Needed Now

swim
INTO THE NORTH'S BLUE EYE

POETRY BY

ANNETTE LAPOINTE

Copyright © 2023 by Annette Lapointe

Library and Archives Canada Cataloguing in Publication

Title: Swim / into the north's blue eye : (poems) / Annette Lapointe.
Other titles: Swim into the north's blue eye | Into the north's blue eye
Names: Lapointe, Annette, 1978- author.
Identifiers: Canadiana 20230450601 | ISBN 9781772142112 (softcover)
Subjects: LCGFT: Poetry.
Classification: LCC PS8623.A728 S95 2023 | DDC C811/.6—dc23

Cover design: Derek von Essen
Cover & interior etching: Paul Lapointe
Interior: HeimatHouse
Represented in Canada by Publishers Group Canada
Distributed by Raincoast Books

The publisher gratefully acknowledges the financial assistance of the Canada Council for the Arts, the Government of Canada, and the Province of British Columbia through the B.C. Arts Council and the Book Publishing Tax Credit.

Anvil Press Publishers Inc.
P.O. Box 3008, Station Terminal
Vancouver, B.C. V6B 3X5 CANADA
www.anvilpress.com

PRINTED AND BOUND IN CANADA

for my friends & relations

These poems were previously published in the following publications:

"the air full of water like insects" in *The Dalhousie Review* as "the air full of water at sea level" (Spring 2022).

"flight" in *The Waggle* magazine (2014).

"fly-in, 1970-74" in *Grain* magazine (2002).

The italicized passage on p. 29 is a quotation from *Crime and Punishment* by Fyodor Dostoyevsky. Translated by David Magarshack. Published by Penguin Books, 1961.

Table of Contents

lilies on the road to île-à-la-crosse

this country leaps from
marsh to forest fire
its gaps pull you miles out
north into bush   rocks
rise out of earth-deep
glacial tarns and show
their petroglyphs

rock ditches spit up colour
where the road turns   you see
earlier crash sites marked
with bicycle reflectors   plastic
carnations weave round the crosses
these few live flowers

more water   more rock lie
at the road's end   islands reach
the shore by ice-roads
blaze in the short summer
leaves fireweed blooming

all along this drive
you read the country
              missives
from the last cold world

when you drive down from edmonton

watch with both eyes

yellowhead highway twists
like a snake moving from under
your wheels   coiling
into tight oncoming brilliance
out into the stillness of aspen woods
from which mule deer
leap and strike

listen for the road

your ears stretch across the river
and out north   colouring
highway danger onto sound
the blue heart of distance

gabriel ferry crossing

every cigarette's smoke curls down
touches the ice   condenses
like the footprint of a breath

you can perch on a river for hours
before the ice breaks under your will
new scum already glistening
by the time you dive

the shock that stops your heart
reveals heaven in the sediment's shift

you swim for miles under the ice
until it gapes open   black
brilliant only in the instant
of your break   the air
like fire smoking your breath

while you crouch in the cold
the water-logs' harrows smooth
any trance of your passage
winter's fingers bind you to the ice

silver

you freeze for months
   and the world opens

ten thousand snowbirds
chime on the ledge
at first light
   sharp tooths of sound that catch
the long, slow lisp
of freezing

this multitude of feathers
white ground
                white sky

＠＠

body of a whole salmon
          buried in ice
someone cradled it
precious as the gift of a heart
all the way from vancouver

you slice it open and the shimmer
of the pacific spills
          over your palms

silver-red entrails an offering
to the spirit of cold life

℗℗

(shell)

remember what an orange smells like
remember how good fruit is in deep winter
    how you can massage it for an hour
      the smell expanding into your skin and hair
      before you breach the rind

    open to me
     oh pen to me
     open to me   open to me open to me   .
     opentome

massaging the skin loose
when even the core gives up what's underneath

      one seed buried in its heart

surgery at the biggar hospital / storm approaching

the shoals of flesh are
what you remember   each breath pours
onto the coralled bed of your abdomen
and stills there   reflecting

spots I've kissed in other hours
slow eyes I dipped into your
navel and lifted   dripping
expectation   I've lived at the bottoms of oceans

and drifted   waiting
for the quick slit of your flesh
in surgery   this stillness channels rain
towards the hospital   it erodes trenches

in the clouds where light
breaks suddenly   catches the glass
of specimens preserved   a floating sargasso
where every jar is the hollow of a life

the chemical bath washes excised
flesh back to its origins
            I could drown in this light's
contained seas   liquid where the sky opens

the ukrainian immigrant thinks of winter

each time you act it out
it's the same

the shape of now twists
and your grandchildren
breast barbed wire and
snow-ridden fields

humid october frozen blurs
lines from the pole until saskatchewan ukraine atlantic
one line
                              you remember the distance
arctic watchtowers clawing
the cloud cover's face

the sex blood insect catch of the wire
lines parallel worlds   the woods seep
between them   you can taste it
the infection bright touching your mouth

the road to yorkton

the rush of water over you is what
you remember on this drive   everything
crouches at grass-level   runs past
liquid green   red   asphalt grey
the continuous yellow-white of the lines
willows swell like
oversoaked fingers at the fringe
of the road allowance

blues pushing down the pavement
clouds pour into
the crevice of tree-channelled road

the trembling rain-wash strips
over the hood   recalls
your last funeral   the last drunken
time you went skinny-dipping
in the south saskatchewan   surfaced
to find it was already dark
                              mosquitoes
rising in long breaths from the mud

how you drifted like a skin boat
seamed by your appendix scar
to the next bend   pushing
down a foot occasionally to rudder yourself
into the current

in the field of this darkening blue
the clutch of dead friends slips
becomes the grass-floe seduction
of your newest love
eyelid of the night pulls open
makes you a skin craft with a steel shell
polished iris of halogen on a dark
warm freshwater sea

frogs at the edge of the yellowhead lunge
into your high beams
                                green-yellow rips
that blink
                that vanish under the tires

flight

you crouch in the frost
and fieldstone gathering
all your sight

and wait   barbed wire
curls down the sand wall
to the ice

cold you barely remember
grows like lichen
loving your stillness

the terns flying north
through this saturation
are sheathed in light

so brilliant
that any single breath
will make them shatter

in the canoe   running

he went out
for days
in the canoe   running
with the current

he painted in mid-stream
the early morning   the rain
softening the paper
his colours in the boat-bottom
mixed with sand
with the water trailing
down his legs

the river shallowed
randomly   sometimes
nearly beaching him   he could
reach down and touch the bottom
inches below the surface

other places
he would drop a glass inkwell
lose it to the deep water

⊚⊚

the barn
          a glass-works
jars of bolts   unmounted windows
marbles in their tobacco bag
suspended from a nail
the scrape of insects climbing
up blue insulators
violet of medicine bottles

he is no more visible
in this than he would be
in the back of a mirror

touch the hydrant rising
out of the barn's dirt
feel the groundwater cold
creasing the iron

loosen the bolt
                    suddenly
he has more water
than vessel to fill

it is this way that
words dissolve
                    they pour
like quicklime into a chemical pail
the rush of water obscures
what you were going to say next

he rises suddenly out of the canoe
dives into the river

the bottom is
twice his body length down
a long breath and exhalation
caught by his impact with the surface
extended in his dive

the water rushing down on him
as he rises

for a quarter of a mile he
swims beside the boat   watches how
the trees bend in their reflections
the stones refract

he lifts himself back in
reaches for the cork-stoppered inkwell
sketches the shoreline
sands that change colour
dissolve where the water touches them
gates that open naturally between the conifers

(studio   early morning)

an inventory of containers:
the liquid bowl
he sinks his hand into
  the ceramic jar of pencils

the unpainted chair that warms
until he can't
distinguish it from his body

stones pooled
at the edge of the table
are remarkable
for their small weights

the den of her winter

the nights hulk with bears

gaping prints they leave
pool with lake water
the claws' curves seeping
acid from conifers

she photographs them   buries
the film   undeveloped
in the den of her winter
blankets and music lining the silence
that shakes her own claws loose

bears unearth caches
pick them over   connoisseurs of salvage
a flashlight gives more entertainment
than a carcass
spare tires merit burial
every light   every shallow road
is a source of fascination

she comes home to find
the screen wire slit   gouged
the kitchen ransacked

every record has been emptied
from its case   the best ones chewed
for remnants of fevered nights
of greasy meat and chocolate

                                    she's left
with echoes of their choices

in the back country   formal barter
for these fragments of vinyl   bears

with her coffee   crouched in chokecherry
make bargains   *two beach boys singles*
for the toothpaste   *johnny cash*
for the secret of fire

you bring me billie holiday
and I'll give you the moon

fly-in   1970-74

she came to Edmonton
by rail the first time
flew out with him
in the pre-dawn
bulked under her parka
                          later
he remembered how
she'd reached for him
in the cold of the station
in the electric
floods of the airstrip

he'd grown up
sleeping in downtown hotels
nights there with his family
two   three in a bed
the air close
like a single-engine otter
in mid-flight

a sherry bottle on the night table
could remind him of his father

◎◎

the paperback dostoyevsky
and a sweater filled her bag,
  (what if instead of all this,
  you suddenly
  find just a little room there
  something like a village bathhouse,
      grimy
  spiders in every corner
  and that's all eternity is)
a pair of his socks for
the flight back

this is the most exciting
part of their early lives
                the involuted
silence of the north broken
by respite trips, the opportunity
to watch your lover
in the bar   dance
with someone else

          at night
the bedspread between them
like a mouth
opened and became
the downtown language
tasting a little
of the snow on jasper avenue
that melted in the small
hours of the morning

north saskatchewan

he woke in nights
made electric by radio
hulked toward the beach
crouched in the shallows
while insects
flooded around him

swept into the lake

stripped by the shape of water
a breath away from crystalline
he touched the bottom
and flipped over

an instant of his feet
breaking surface
before he leapt down

rose into air thick with wings
clouds of fish
feeding at the edges of his reach

one drowned world
bordered the other

ichthya

fish made the world

deep under
where the eye is least important
they found and swallowed rocks
surfaced with them
rattling in cages
of flesh and flexible bone

opened and left them on shore
dove while the second
world expanded

long slow sounds
rang outward
new forms entered the world
a stone   a snowmobile
a mammalian body sinking

cold hearts echoed
the dream of flight   insects
captured in a moment of brilliance
sang back for months
stories of air and fire

cold expanded
and the world darkened

while they dozed among
glacial rocks
heavens of ice shifted

bush work

he works in the heat and light
his rope horse in old harness   dozing
at the bush's edge   waits for him to sight
the tree and cull it   aspen

trees hold the world in place   they trap
the earth   hold salt lakes off
the slough a mile away sings frogs
and water   sinking under   flowing up

groundwater fails and trees die
bare white arms in the aspen's water-tangle
call out to birds and fire
burn this   the wood here hangs

until the lightning hits   the waiting storm
licks wet electric wind   leaves out the rain
until a cigarette falls from a car
window   blows in across the wire

he crawls in through the chokecherry
and wild rose briar   armed
with chainsaw and horse he lays in   carves
then pulls til the wood falls free

they haul out logs   three green tons
lounge in the barn's shadow   six
weeks' work   then split and stack
it up against the wind
                          the pile leans back

through this absence of darkness

(campsell portage   hepatitis   1971)

in this fevered month
there are new poisons

nights when her organs twist
fluids out of sleep
when she craves honey
insects   real fruit
she swears never to eat another rabbit
when their heads are discovered
preserved in the deep freeze

the edge of the snow
holds her   cavernous in blankets
breathing away nausea

ice crusting her skin
sweeps between layers of fur
and fat
chills her organs
to the stillness of glaciers

he takes her picture   she arches
turns on her side
re-enters her book   when he passes
she locks him
in the pitch of her glass
her mouth soaking one hip
while the spilled rum trails
down his leg

dark courses
                    through the winter

he tastes her whenever he wakes
erect in the cold to piss
into the night's lens
the bruises she marked on him
slit the stillness   aching sounds
loud enough to touch

she's phosphorescent
lightless months rendered her a glittering
peripheral danger
when he looks at her directly
she sears his retinas
buries his eye's flesh
in nails of daylight

she crawls out of the lake
enters a winter country
swimming in shallow light

insects float
on her drying arms into the house
she traps them in a tumbler
patterns the rest of her day
against their echoes

sleep at 2 a.m.   the sun
breathing through the blind's fingers
into the room
          the world twists
through this absence of darkness
breaking on sleep's edge

at 6 she makes tea
pushes through blackfly curtains
to the lake

if she dropped her cup and dove now
she could find him
the wave of mosquitoes
when she rises
as frantic as his touch

hepatitis 2   1973

this winter breaks   the swelling

heaves earth & bodies
soaks infectious
memories from walls

when she walks   each draft
pulls outward   crawls between
the sawdust and asbestos
loose in darkness with the rock
thrust up

this silica and sleeve ice   they reflect
her boots   the breathless
skiff of winter paws
awake and hunting
these chained dogs
lurk and strike
growl through bloody feasting
starve between their catches

the fruit she dreams of
hulks in crates   her scurvy grows
cirrhosis   slow organ
failure transforming flesh
other beings hunting
in her brain
                    between the humours
and the bone   the ice outside
new lives begin and end

not everything you know
is absolute   your hair slips free
from fingers and your scalp
your liver calls up
poisons in your blood

each insect in the woodpile wakes
and dies before it hits the ground

if she descended

      he takes her picture

the light behind her swells
smears the negative
so afterwards she's faceless
overwritten by the light

outside   the ice
carves spring/march brilliance
into layers
           sheets of it
whisper along the rock faces

in the early morning,
he takes pictures of the ice

he flies out to edmonton
hitches rides to vancouver

crashes with friends
on hawks avenue   the chinese
red of the house
an inundation

in the bathroom the first
morning he sluices
off accumulated
cold and altitude

goes walking, he
buys sandalwood soap
on union street

red paper wrappers
their gold seals more vivid
than a year in the snow

◎◎

he cracks open his luggage
her glasses are there
offered like a vulva
between two folded jean-legs

he remembers them
within the frame of her hair

one lens in his shirt pocket
cups his right nipple
damp as the rain increases

in stanley park
the arms unfold
slip wet and open towards him

impossibly heavy
as if the glass were her whole body

staring across burrard inlet
red plaid soaking
from his shirt to his skin
he looks through them

the world distorts
into something entirely hers

he comes over the bridge
vaults the last step
from muskeg to rock

newly disturbed lichens
crawl up his shoes
        nest
in the hollows of his laces

this is
        a new forest
all its geese
were washed by the pacific
onto the rocks
and marooned   beggars
whose black tongues
shriek at approaching cars

this cedar forest
locked in vancouver
lives in the hearts of geese

their feathers
a second ocean
just above the first

if she descended —

he imagines quills
rising to meet her
a stretch of wings
from english bay
to the soft earth behind him

she walks toward him
on water too saline
to let her submerge

not cold enough to drown

ucluelet   1974

he comes to the rim of the world
and the trees he finds are small
cousins to the shelled white logs
where the earth's shelf curls under

green density of the forest's face
less startling than these bones' protection
against the pacific's explosive breath

spray curves in and names the shape
of the moon's diurnal bump
that knocks the seas into rising

echoes the speaking curl
of his own breath   he takes drifted
branches   builds a frame of her body

stretching twice his height   climbs
it to coif the mute wet sea-shapes
of kelp   of the island's cathedral moss

all day he sits beside it   soaking outwards
the bone coins of the frame's nails
scratch at the spreading humidity

ice shards graft to his hair
twelve hundred miles across the earth's breast
she sighs out frost in her sleep
arches   curls toward him

sea level

he remembers the swell of her breast
the sheltered glass door
carving her shape into the light

seven islands
between vancouver and saskatoon

he buries offerings to her
everywhere he stops

dreams her in the ringing glass
world of the pacific

@@

he could swim here

the grass thunders
islands thrust up trees
prehistoric bivalves
swell open   licking wetness
from the night

this morning
still drunk
he snaps a towel
over his head

the air's flood
                    new wings

sea witch

she remembers salt as if it were oceans
instead of alkali flats
                              those early
dreams she confuses with trips
her mother's arms and waist
thigh-deep in english bay
some early family lower mainland pilgrimage

that single ocean's salt
          and it's salt she remembers
even in this sand ground she can taste it

there are shallow rivers here
one hundred fifty feet below the topsoil
sliding upward into centreless marshland

the only blackbirds she can name
are slough messengers   red-winged
water seekers   rising at the first vibration
any foot that shakes the earth's crust

∾∾

her grandmother points to the moon
but she feels groundwater
                              like the tension
in her cunt   the water vibrates
hollow in a way she can't yet voice

when she stretches
she can feel her wet heart tear

◎◎

in the space between sunshine
and intimate breath
she drowns with her feet in shallow water

pulling at the current
                                she remembers
this more clearly than drowning

her first step into the channel
swallowed sound and light
silt caught in the undertow greened
her first breathless fall
from the river flats into deep water
        every liquid moment caught
        between her skins
                                swelled up
        and pushed her to the surface

⚙⚙

it's the shock
the moment your heart stops
the water's echoes
shape your gut to the ice's
gouged-out memory of shale

this northern water is acidic   pools of trees
submerged and melting
tint the light
                she kicks
and blows, deflating even hollows
of her lungs   thrusts deeper
touches cliffs

the centre bottoms out of reach

this water clutches at her traces

every alkaline lick of her can change
            one current's pattern
crack a stone face into pools

these springs are new
                        they edge
between the strengths rock offers
salting memory in shallow
curves of ice   each winter follows
out the surfaces she touched

decommission

he comes down from alaska
decommissioned
strung out on wires

                                  from the bering ice

each radio an echo in his skull

planes he loved
resonate
          even in sleep
the ringing never stops

the prairie he lands on
shudders at a touch
thin crusts above the water table
carry sound into bedrock
break it open
send it back

he wakes singing holiday
her voice tympanic pain
in the limited space before morning

     liquid in the daylight
pouring over him while he dresses

@@

the days he goes out ploughing the
sandhills liquid ground
farm machines
wrap white noise around his hearing
       growling diesel engines scar him   ringing
       drives her voice
                    (holiday's voice and her voice
overlapping his brain)
behind the drum

sound stops

૭૭

his deafness mutes every
voice but radio

nights he wraps crystal
around his heart and listens to the air

he dreams of planes and forests
radio and water   air
like a sudden ice rush going forth
from the lips of his shell
the glaciers contained
in songs
                in static

@@

he can't always remember what country
he's in when he wakes

barracks on the beach in alaska /
        cabin in the stone belt of the north /
farm in the prairie's swell

unfinished boards in both
        naked glass marked by insects
canned oysters and his
shoulders spreading out wings

going out to the creek house
                he can hear
the ocean in the grass moving
        in the islands defined by trees

his split foot's twinge
sings to him oysters   sex
the ocean's memory and
her breasts like animals
(birds   insects)
        swimming in the night

steam ships grinding past against their rails
moan her breath/body back into his eye

⊚⊚

she keeps his wings in a jar
every avian moment
shudders in the glass
invisible to the eye
it moves outward, drifting
toward the moment the glass slides
downward   until it
finally dissolves

◎◎

these days of travel
two of rain
        two of steaming cold
the early-morning stillness
of the float-plane's flight

metamorphosis in the humid
shell of the car

north through the mackenzie range
to the black glassed basalt
of the world's north rim

under the road
there are turns that swallow breath

one corroded sign —
vision limited

the circumspection
of expansive ground

℗℗

circuitous return

anchorage to panama
mexico city to havana
baja california to seattle
seattle to vancouver
to saskatoon

       stopped by harris (saskatchewan)
for air
she breathes in insects with the dryness

thinks of his wings

night birds

these are nights she dreams of moving
air   sand mites bathing
in the cleft of her spine
            her sweat and the insects
            crawl across her sleep

all night she curls around
sirens and engines
the street noise
curves sleep's surface

their skins are detailed by a shout
between the air and insects screens
shake voices into wire

she retains that want
her slick around him
the line of his back   his leg
hairs sharp against her shaved
thigh

            she knows his smell
this isn't him
                    the flare
of shoulder blade is different
he has scars she can't recall
she sleeps against his shape
uneasily   folds more comfortably
without him

outside there are wings on wire
the trees and lines
all catch at magpies
swarming above the insects' reach
their blood is less a smell than sound
each whisper is a heart

one wing dreams out of sequence
it wakes shouting   falling
catches on a branch
rouses every breathing bird
he scrapes and sits stark upright
cracked open by the noise
shaking his own heart loose

insect winds across his face
brush weakness under skin and sheets
the fear slides off him

she tilts her hips toward him
he reads alarm across her breasts
one worried shoulder
    looking outward

they hear birds scream
before they settle

in this wing-enfolded stillness she forgets
love's shallow spread across the dark

like the opening of a shell

turning over watermarked pages
from the time I fell asleep
by the pool
        being startled
awake and dropping my book
into the water

not the only thing
I had to dive for but
the only one in danger of dissolving

what else have I dropped?
my glasses   my chain necklace
while I was swimming
                    sometimes
my place-memory

kicking deep
closed my hand around
a child's pearl bracelet made of
heathered plastic   each bead
like the opening of a shell

expecting to surface in a world
delineated by bamboo
rather than chokecherry

ceremonial aspen

oracy

this is
　　　　nothing written
it has been
done or taken
by the mouth

you have to be
　　　　　　empty first

spoken examination

I can tell you what snow
tastes like
                  bone
what it tastes
like the hardness in water
tastes
it tastes pain
          white scraping through teeth
          and mouth
making
what it tastes like
                  skin

⊚⊚

how it imitates the
motions of eating
peeling and tasting
the juice that leaks out of
         the skin

how it
segments the fruit
sucking it gently
a moment before
ripping out the centre
with its tongue

◎◎

this is done
by word of
mouth

subvocal
preliterate
unwritten

      it is what
passes from the lips and
fills

morning moon

morning moon

                                                              snow

god that blue what do I call it
    shadow
four days to the new year
headlights and all these grouse
on the road   a deer maybe

red christmas lights
    and miles   all farmsteads
arced around this road

this is farthest
   point from you love
your asia mountainstowerswater
I remember the fields and the road
down south to your city

@@

morning moon
                                                                    ceramic

goldfish chipped   half-buried in the garden
six years of drought   two floating
rain's always there   expected
(weeks   days after weeks
            this almost-desert)

fish swims
it needs pools   puddles
mud at least to burrow down

I have these mornings
nightgown and barefoot
                        with the hose
making the fine spray

come on   swim
            breathe

∾

morning moon

                                         salamander

crouch and think about the coast
its marshes
even here
water's mixed with alkali salt

sweating in the light   blue
still wind at ground level
small noises   water and the sucking feet
of amphibious creatures over
pool and paving granite

you wait months
                to lie here
think of fire
how their colours explode
        as they dive

@@

morning moon

                                                        dog

sleep on the floor in seoul
laid-open skill pools this summer
back to the air conditioner   knees up
dog's nose under my breast

stretching four a.m. light is clean
blue as the day isn't
          smog's out to sea
          rain's broken

sundressed   barefoot
walking in the alley
some noise twists and I catch
sun's white reflection between towers

me and the dog
               both looking up

⊚⊚

morning moon

                                                               wire

owls in the grey snow
    hour-long commute in back country
you rise over the road
catch their daybreak hunting

   wings like breaths

fences here to saskatoon
          snag them
shadows   we drive through
bare trees   savaged feathers

@@

morning moon

                                                        eye

the road is full of mirrors
look to the passenger's window
light comes to you
from miles ahead

you lose distances
but judge carefully
        you'll never strike

travel across the continent
watch for animals
never look at the pavement
                only at the glass

equinox

the first rain is what you dream of
it builds in faint masses   breathes
up from moulded ground layers
water rises out of its buried
sloughs to fill the air

we calculated   drunk in the basement
the moment we could stand a raw egg
on its end

driving at night   loose dust
clapped over the pavement   the car hood
   applauded across the windshield
like a scar   tonight
the engine beats against the hood
  oiled heart that pushes loose

                              car's one-eyed
lights trace frost damage in the road
running up fantasies   fragments of my last kiss
melting from tongue music
into light   a catalogue of loves
brought into balance

my grandfather's dog who snatched fish out of the
athabasca river   my father
who nursed that dog
years past his father's death

                            my aunt and uncle
who split their possessions
into two camps   brooded over them a month
in a house divided

last summer   august night   how the
dragonfly's penis reached back in a perfect
arc of aerial mating

lake static

soaps sound through the house
unillustrated since the death of the
vertical hold   television
measures the daylight
even floating on the lake   passions
drift out to me
herons plot
liaisons in the bush

I've stayed up nights
listening
to the dog circle claw marks
around the kitchen table

waiting for you to show
like a nighttime dog
snuffling around patio doors
2 a.m. visitor who crawls
wet-furred and half-welcome
onto the covers

two single beds pushed together
so my fingers can brush
over your spine   the chasm between
mattresses is a throat that
swallows limbs

rattle and hum

curl of silverfish in the basement
books swell and breathe
a carpet of paper along the cement
five weeks it's been raining
primitive life leaks through
settles in the lower shelves

an education's worth of joyce
being slowly consumed by insects

nights we slept here
swallowing
the rattle of thunder
with the paperbacks' demise

naked legs through the house   my feet
shaping the layers of books
the soft shells of desiccated insects
swept under the ledge of the last stair
even the curl of a grub
soaked since last year in tequila
expands into an umbilical   knowing eel

radio's flicker cuts apart soft wood
layers of glass   old paper
the signal eaten for half-minute stretches
by swelling damp that corrodes the wires
by abandoned carapaces
that make the transistors a second shell

upstairs   the kitchen porch full of bottles
its screen exposed to moving air
that beats
          through the wings of a fan
wings of small moths
catch on the wire

their chipped reflections strike
the sheet stretched along the couch
the chewed-out heart of a lime

      each static charge creates
      radiance in the shell of the door

finches and orchids in season

in the hours after it rains
they burst from the ground

warped by the cyclic arid intervals
        the enzymes begging
their new colours —
pine red and evening
yellow grosbeak

orange as a gene-spliced
multi-tongued many winged
hybrid
bird and flower are one

the orchids chime lemon-pink
voices in their glass frames

finches nest in decomposing
trees   they dig in parasitic feet
crawl into combustion's warmth
they change by hours
their eggs   revealed to dim eyes
                        have tongues
show seed beneath the skin
their shells translucent

too thick to catch fire

moisture in this room like wet incense —
the windows all open   the air is
too thick to catch fire

rain demands the depths of a garden
a shelter from the street noises

a low roof
to throw the water off

the smell of it comes pouring
around the ceramic jars
the wood rim of the pond

this mix of quiet and loud water
becomes the most important feature
of the night

vancouver layover   seoul to saskatoon

eighteen years of childhood
desert and the rains trap you

water's not for steps
or drenching

you watch it build
the seacoasts washed for months

still you count
quarters of inches   breaths

falling   it waits for you
marks each open window

as you listen for
six drops that break the night

the air full of water like insects

you promised to go swimming with me
when the rains ended

days waiting

I want you like loud water
            pulling
at my fingers
everything I write is
of you
            immersed

my last dream
was of walking through libraries
and opening books
            the water bowl on the table
had your face in it

layover   second day

you lie
years in saskatchewan
vancouver an oasis
at your rim

those rains
debauch you   make
pavilions out of porches
satin wood grain
in your touch

and this   is
babylon   its waters
honey fruit   give
sea life up to plates
you eat orchids
this dark is
winter closing
flowers in your jaw

you live in desert
     jealous   flat
and wind-voiced
howling
          snow locks
honey from the heart

and this
your monster crawls
each winter to the
west   it sings
pacific   all your nights
you wake up hungry

north sandhills

the earth caves open
and a new mouth
laps the air
its throat dives

white and root-haired
to the water table,
singing stopless liquid
memories of ice

sounds catch on each
protruding tooth
on bones knocked loose
by the ground's shift

called to this depth
this was a well
   the house dissolved
to just the crafted

frames of windows
water and a hand
reach for the door
describing echoes

two bodies buried
in unconsecrated ground
stripped by sand
slide towards the shaft

each winter swallows them
new tilts of earth
new lights raise fractured
music from the bottom

Acknowledgements

This collection owes so much to the mentorship of Carole Itter and Daphne Marlatt. Thank you both for your invaluable guidance.

Thank you to melanie brannagan frederiksen for her editor's eye, for her years of friendship, and for telling me what the title should be.

Thank you to my husband John, for his companionship and almost infinite patience.

And thanks to my parents for sharing the stories of their families and of their own lives, for travelling with me, and for guiding me through the process of seeing.

About the Author

Annette Lapointe (she/her) lived in rural Saskatchewan, Quebec City, St John's, Saskatoon, Winnipeg, and South Korea before settling in northern Alberta. She now lives in Treaty 8 territory and teaches English and creative writing at Northwestern Polytechnic. She is the author of three acclaimed novels (*Stolen, Whitetail Shooting Gallery, ...And This is the Cure*) and a collection of short stories (*You Are Not Needed Now*). Her website is www.annettelapointe.com.